Rahab's Red Thread

Joshua 2
for children

Written by Erik Rottmann

Illustrated by Linda Pierce

CONCORDIA PUBLISHING HOUSE · SAINT LOUIS

God sent His people Israel
Into the Promised Land.
God told His servant Joshua,
"Now you are in command."

So Joshua chose two brave men.
He told them both to go
And find out what was happening
Inside of Jericho.

A girl named Rahab met these men.
She hid them from her king.
He tried to catch the two of them
By searching everything.

With courage Rahab risked her life
To save these hunted spies.
She told them that she feared the Lord.
That's why she helped them hide!

She told them how she'd heard the word
Of God's amazing deed,
How up from Egypt God had brought
His people through the sea.

She'd heard how God had toppled kings
And swore to give this land
To His dear people Israel
With His almighty hand.

Now Israel had come to crush
The city and its wall.
So Rahab begged the spies to save
Her family, one and all.

"Please give a special gift to me,
A token or a sign.
Please give me certainty that you
Will keep me on your mind."

These men from Joshua could see
The Law had done its job
Of causing Rahab to cry out
For mercy from her God.

So Rahab heard a different word,
A promise from the Lord.
They swore that Rahab would be saved.
They offered her a cord.

The cord these men gave to their friend
Was little more than thread.
It was not long and was not strong,
But just a rope of red.

When Jericho and its great wall
Came tumbling to the ground,
The cord reminded Rahab that
She would be safe and sound.

The cord kept Rahab firm in faith.
The cord kept Rahab's eyes
Focused on the faithful Word
That she heard from the spies.

God also gives to you a sign,
More certain than red thread,
That He shall cleanse you from your sins
And raise you from the dead.

Your sign is water joined to Word.
Baptism is its name.
This sign will keep you firm in faith,
Like Rahab, just the same.

Like Rahab's thread, your Baptism
Will help you when you fear.
It ties you to your risen Lord,
Who faithfully stays near.

Dear Parents

"Baptism . . . now saves you" (1 Peter 3:21). Use *Rahab's Red Thread* to help your child understand how Baptism gives God's gift of salvation. The spies gave Rahab a simple piece of red cord. By itself, the cord had no ability to save Rahab and her family. However, the spies attached a powerful promise to the cord: "We will deal kindly and faithfully with you," they said. "Tie this scarlet cord in the window" (Joshua 2:14, 18). This red cord was a sign for the Israelites who invaded Jericho. It showed them that Rahab and her family should be protected and not harmed. But this red cord also was a comforting reminder for Rahab that the spies had spoken a promise to her. Every time she looked at the red cord, Rahab could remember their promise!

Every day, you and your child can look the same way at God's gift of Baptism. Like the red cord, the water itself does not wash away your sins, remove the curse of death, or give you eternal salvation. Rather, it is God's powerful, miracle-producing Word of promise, joined to the water, that does these things for you. Common and ordinary thread or common and ordinary water: your merciful Lord has attached to baptismal water even greater assurance and comfort for you and for your child than was attached to Rahab's red thread.

The Author